ABOUT FIRST LOOK BOOKS

A new series designed to teach young readers the fundamentals of computer operation and programming, First Look Books are an ideal resource for parents, teachers and students. Ideas are developed logically, from simple computer concepts to the complexities of the binary number system and programming. Illustrated with dozens of lively drawings, each of the First Look Books helps the young reader progress in learning about computers and how they work.

Each First Look Book may be enjoyed individually or as one in a series.

BOOKS IN THE "FIRST LOOK" SERIES

FIRST LOOK BOOK #1
COMPUTERS: Sizes, Shapes and Flavors
by J.M. Johnston

FIRST LOOK BOOK #2
COMPUTERS: Beeps, Whirs and Blinking Lights
by J.M. Johnston

FIRST LOOK BOOK #3
COMPUTERS: Menus, Loops and Mice
by J.M. Johnston

COMPUTERS
Sizes, Shapes and Flavors

COMPUTERS
Sizes, Shapes and Flavors

J. M. Johnston

A Dell/Banbury Book

Published by
Miles Standish Press, Inc.
353 West Lancaster Avenue Wayne, Pennsylvania 19087

Dell ® TM 681510, Dell Publishing Co., Inc.

ISBN: 0-440-01375-5

First printing — August 1983

10 9 8 7 6 5 4 3 2

For Arne

They're here. They're there. All around! They're almost everywhere.

Invaded? Well . . . sort of.
But it's a *friendly* invasion.
I'm talking about *computers*.

I don't see any computers.

Oh, but that doesn't mean they're not there. You can't see your heart, either, can you? But you know it's there, because it's pumping blood around in your body and keeping you alive. And you can't see your brain, but if it weren't there you couldn't think very well. And you can't see—

Okay, okay. But I know where my brain and heart are. Where are these computers you keep talking about?

Why, they're in airplanes, telephones, watches, hospitals, kitchen stoves, factories, rockets, motorcycles, libraries, traffic lights, schools, television sets, gas stations, grocery stores, clocks, light switches, hearing aids, sewing machines, toasters, toothbrushes—

Well . . . okay, maybe not toothbrushes. But subways, exercise machines, bathroom scales, police cars, typewriters, microscopes, lawnmowers—

Hey, wait a minute. You say computers are in all these places. But I thought computers were big boxes, with a television screen and somebody sitting down and typing things on a sort of typewriter. How do you get all that in a light switch, or a hearing aid?

Aha! What you're talking about is only one kind of computer. But computers come in all sizes, shapes and flavors. Big ones that take up a whole room, and tiny ones that can fit on your fingernail. Some you can carry around with you, some come in kits. Some are right out in the open, and some are hidden away where you'd never find them, in places you'd never think to look.

Well, I guess that's why I don't see any.

Would you like to see some? Go to those places where computers are, and see what they do and how they do it?

Well...

Come on. Trust me.

Hmm. . . . that's what my father says when we take a trip and he wants to try a new short cut. But okay. Let's go. Show me these computers. Where do we go first?

How about the hospital? Ah, here we are. Now what is the first thing you see as we go into the lobby?

A man in a wheelchair.

No, no—I mean over there at the receptionist's desk.

Right. It's a *computer terminal.* As we will see later, a computer terminal is what allows us to talk to a computer, and allows the computer to give us information.

A computer terminal is like a typewriter, only better. A typewriter can't print anything unless we type on the keys. But a computer terminal can.

And it's a little like a television set, too, except that a television set only talks to *us*—we can't talk back to *it.* A computer terminal can do both. It's also like talking on the telephone, except that our conversation is printed instead of spoken.

What is she typing on the terminal?

She's typing information about the patients in the hospital—things like their names and addresses, when they came into the hospital, what was wrong with them, and which rooms they are in. These are called the patients' *files*.

Later, someone will add more information to these files, like the kinds of medicine they have to take and how often they have to take them. Or special foods they must eat, and foods they shouldn't eat.

Now, the computer remembers all this information in the files. Suppose a doctor or nurse needs to know what time Mrs. Jones is supposed to get a pill, or whether Mr. Smith is allowed to have salt with his meal. They type in their questions on the terminal, and the computer finds the answer in its files and prints it on the screen.

Where is the computer? Is it in the terminal with the screen?

No, although some computers and their terminal screens are all together in one box. The hospital computer is somewhere else in the building and there are lots of terminals like this one hooked up to it.

So lots of people can ask it questions.

Right. There's a terminal in each nurses' station, in the laboratory where tests are done, and even in some doctors' offices.

What kinds of tests are done in the laboratory?

Well, let's go in and take a look, shall we?

See all those bottles, test tubes and chemicals? These are all used to test fluids and tissue samples from patients to see if they show anything wrong.

There's the computer terminal over there. Besides being able to answer questions about the patients, this one can actually run the tests I mentioned. It measures a patient's blood pressure, temperature, pulse and breathing to decide if they are normal.

Some are even smarter. A doctor can use another terminal to type in the symptoms a patient has—like headaches, dizziness, sore throat—and the computer can tell the doctor what kinds of diseases that patient might have. It might even suggest what kind of treatment the patient should have.

Now, look in that room over there. What do you see?

A man is lying in bed and there are wires connected to pads on his chest.

That's right. And those wires are sending information about the man's heartbeat directly to the computer. The computer then draws a pattern of this heartbeat on a terminal screen and a nurse can watch it in a different room.

If the heartbeat changes, the pattern changes, and the nurse can decide whether or not the man needs attention. If his heart starts to have serious trouble, the computer will send an alarm to alert the doctors and nurses, who will quickly come and help him. This watching over a patient by the computer is called *monitoring*. Do you know what a monitor is?

Sure. At school we have class monitors who make sure everyone behaves, and they report trouble to the teacher.

That's exactly what the computer does here—it makes sure the patients stay comfortable and healthy, and reports any problems to the person in charge.

Now in this room—

Wow! What's that big machine shaped like a doughnut?

That is a special type of X-ray machine called an *axial tomography scanner*. You know about X-rays, don't you?

Close enough. Well, this machine takes lots of X-ray pictures of some part of the body—usually the brain. That's why it's doughnut-shaped: it has to go completely around the patient.

Then a computer puts all those different pictures together, like a jigsaw puzzle, so that the doctors can look at the diseased area from all sides.

Just like opening up the top of the head and peeking inside.

Indeed it is, but without surgery. This gives them much more information about how serious the problem is, and how to correct it.

And that's the whole reason for computers in the hospital—the more information a doctor has about patients, the better the chances of finding a cure. A doctor needs the information fast, and without mistakes, because human lives are at stake.

Now, let's go on to another place that uses computers to help protect lives. . . .

A police station?

Absolutely. Computers make crime-fighting a lot easier and faster.

See all those patrol cars lined up over there? Each one of them has a small computer inside. Whenever the driver sees a suspicious car, he types in its license plate number. Then the computer tells him whether or not the car is stolen or belongs to someone with a criminal record.

Or if the policeman arrests someone, the computer in his car can tell him right away if that person is wanted by the police in another state.

But how does the computer know all this?

Let's take a look inside the police station and maybe we'll find out. See anything that looks familiar?

Right. They use the terminals to give the computer information that they will need to use later. What kind of information do you think the police would like the computer to remember?

Well, the license numbers you talked about. And I guess all the stuff about people who are wanted by the police.

Correct. And that's a lot of information. There are thousands of license numbers that the police need to know. And for each criminal, the computer has to know when and where he was arrested, and what he was arrested for. It even keeps fingerprints.

Sure. You know how the police take a person's fingerprints when he's arrested? Well, this computer has a device called a *scanner* which can look at fingerprint pictures and store all kinds of information about them.

Look closely at your fingers—see all those tiny lines that curve and loop around? Each person's are different and the computer will remember those things that make them different. So when a burglar leaves fingerprints, the computer can look at them and determine if they match those of a known criminal.

If I were a burglar, I'd wear gloves!

Ah, but the computer can store lots of other things that help the police identify a person. Voices, for example.

You mean it has scanners for voices, too?

In a way. Computers can make a "print" of your voice, which looks a little like those heartbeat pictures we saw in the hospital. Each person's voice is as distinctive as his fingerprints. The computer will still detect the pattern even if you try to disguise your voice by talking through a handkerchief—

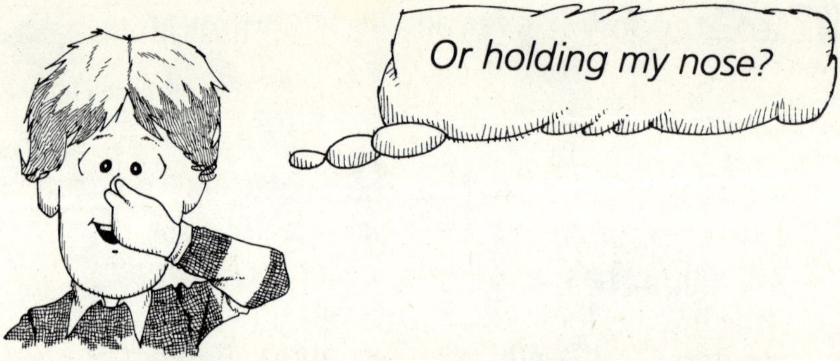

Even that. And the more information the computer has about a person, the easier it will be to identify him.

But the computers here do more than just keep information. See that man with the microphone next to his terminal?

Yes.

He's a *dispatcher.* He receives calls from the patrol cars and tells them where to go when a crime has been reported. The computer helps him do this by figuring out where each patrol car is at any given time. It can even decide which patrol cars are closest to the crime.

What if there aren't any patrol cars nearby?

Then the computer figures out which patrol cars from somewhere else can get there the fastest. Usually, at least one car is only minutes away from the scene of a crime.

In fact, that's another way the computer can help. It also keeps information about where each crime happens. Then it decides which parts of the city are most likely to have trouble.

So it sets up a schedule for each patrol car to follow so that those areas receive the most protection. It even changes the schedules a little bit each day, so a person planning a crime never knows exactly when a police car will show up.

Pretty smart.

It has to be. The police would rather prevent crimes than have to solve them after they've happened.

But can the computer help solve crimes, too?

Certainly. We've already seen how it can identify fingerprints and voices. And remember the laboratory at the hospital?

Yes—where the computer figured out what diseases a person has and what the doctor should do.

Right. And there's a lab here, too. That equipment over there is used to identify substances found at the scene of a crime—like stains, pieces of cloth or hair, or things that may have been used to pry open a window or safe, or set a fire. Or even a murder weapon. It has been used to identify the typewriter that a kidnapper used to write a ransom note and to trace the store where a gun was bought.

And much of this equipment is connected to a computer to make the job easier and faster.

What if a police station doesn't have a computer to do all these things?

Almost all of them do now. And their computers can even talk to each other over telephone lines, so if one doesn't have a certain piece of information, another one might.

Gee—a criminal doesn't have a chance against these computers.

Well, they keep on trying. But it's getting harder and harder to get away with it. Ready for the next stop?

Look at all those big tanks and pipes. They contain chemicals that have to be kept at exactly the right temperature and pressure. They have to flow at exactly the right speed through the pipes and fill the tanks to just the right level.

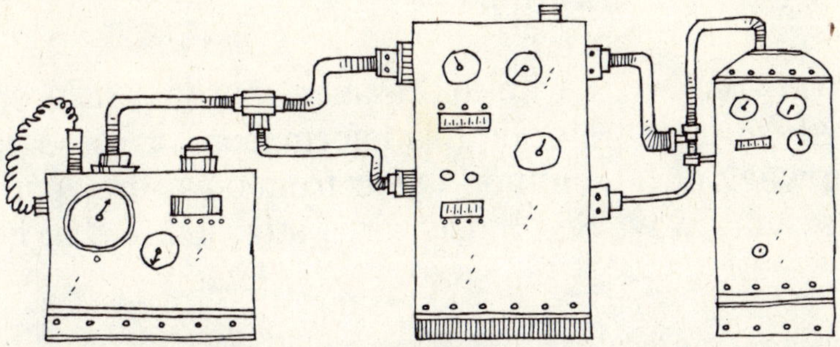

As you probably guessed, this is a *chemical plant,* which produces many of the products we use every day—soaps, plastics, paints, paper, fertilizers, film—even clothes and medicines.

All those things are made here?

Not at this *particular* plant. Each product is usually made at a separate plant. This is just one of hundreds of different kinds of factories which use raw materials to produce the things that make our lives more comfortable. What other kinds of factories can you think of?

Well . . . steel mills?

Sure. And how about oil and coal refineries?

And saw mills.

And sugar refineries and textile plants. And lots more. Some are big, like this one, and some are much smaller. But they all have one thing in common . . .

Computers!

Right. And how do you suppose computers are used here?

Well . . . I guess they store information, like hospitals and police stations. But I'm not sure what kind of information.

Yes, they do work with information, but in a different way. Instead of just storing this information for someone to use a week or a month or a year from now, they put it to work right away. See those wires attached to that big tank?

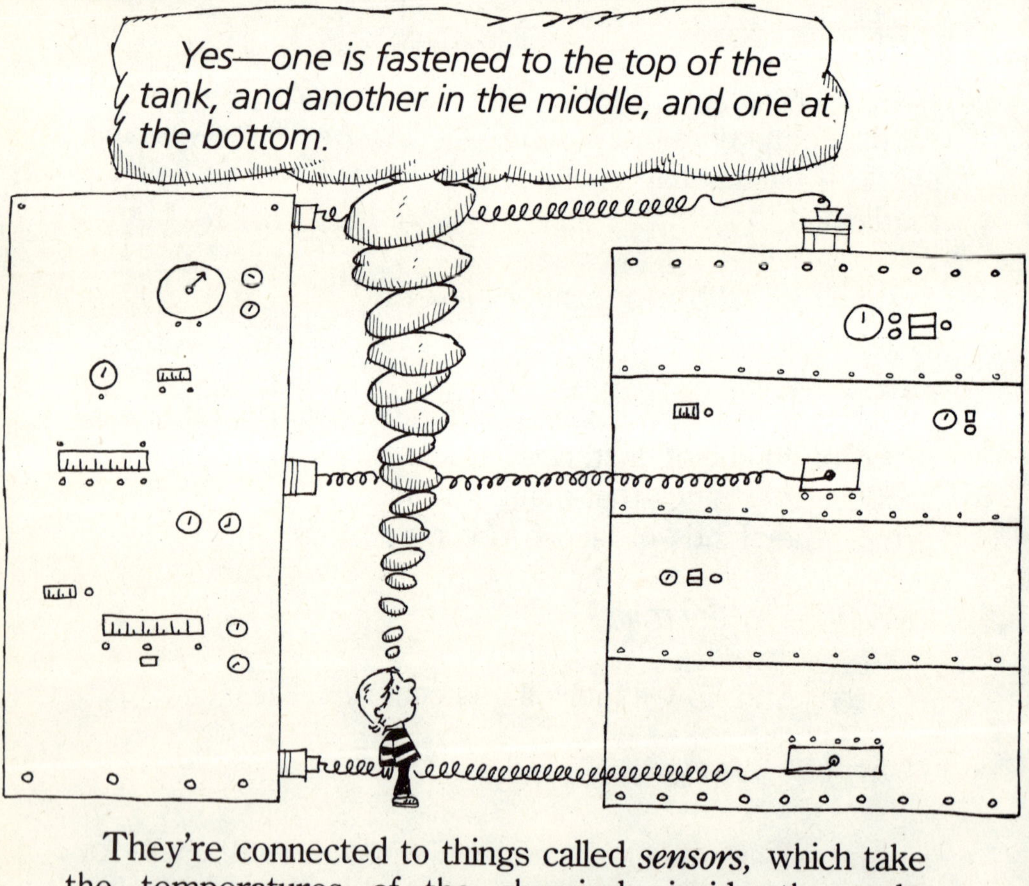

They're connected to things called *sensors,* which take the temperatures of the chemicals inside the tank. Sensors are like the thermometers you put under your tongue when you have a fever. The temperature information is sent through those wires to the computer.

What does the computer do with them?

Well, let's go over and take a look. See that big terminal screen with the lines and numbers in different colors?

Yes—and some parts of it are flashing and changing colors!

The computer is drawing a picture of what's happening inside that tank and displaying it on the screen so that the engineers can tell if the temperature is what it should be.

Just like the man in the hospital with the wires attached to his chest so that they could watch his heart!

Correct. Those were sensors, too. But the computer here does even more.

If the temperature in the tank is too low, the computer sends a signal *back* out through a different wire and causes a heater to come on inside the walls of the tank. If the temperature is too high, the computer's signal turns the heater off.

This is called *process control,* since the computer is controlling the process, instead of just storing information about it.

Then the people don't have anything to do!

Sure they do. They may decide they want to try a higher or lower temperature. So they type a command to the computer and it sends the signal to turn the heater on or off.

Can the computer control anything else besides the temperature?

Sure. There are other sensors in the tank that measure how full the tank is. So if the computer sees that the tank is getting empty, it sends a signal to open a faucet to let more chemicals in.

Or if it gets too full—

Then it sends a different signal to close the faucet.

Now when this happens, the color picture on the terminal screen will change. That green rectangle represents the tank and the yellow line going across the top of it shows how full the tank is. It will be near the top if the tank is full, or close to the bottom when the tank is almost empty.

And if the temperature inside is too high, the color of the rectangle will change from green to red. If it's too low, the color will change to blue.

That's a mixing tank, where several kinds of chemicals are blended together. Can you guess what the computer controls there?

Sure—it has to make sure there's the right amount of each chemical going into the tank.

Right. And when the tank calls for a different combination, the computer opens the faucet on that pipe a little or closes the faucet on another one.

And all this time, the computer is remembering each change that's made, and when it was made, so that the engineers can get this information later.

Just like the doctors and police.

Exactly. Now as I said before, this is only *one* kind of factory. In oil refineries, the computers can control the amount of oil that flows through the pipes. In power plants they control the amount of water that turns the turbines and how much electricity is sent out through the power lines.

In glass factories, the temperature of the molten glass has to be carefully controlled. And in clothing and textile plants, computers control almost everything, including the design of the clothes, measuring and cutting the fabric, and sewing the pieces together.

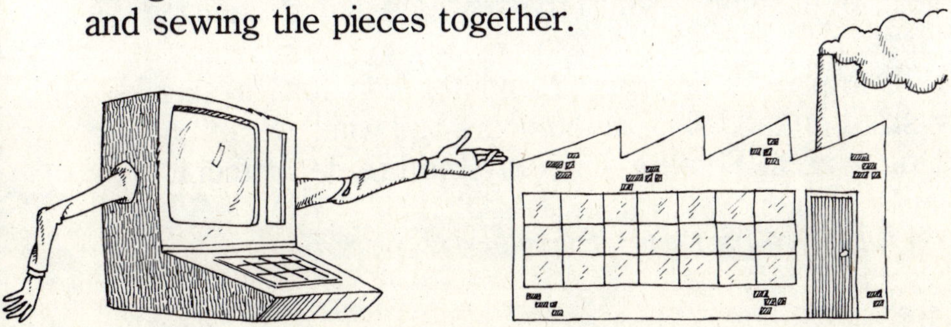

Now, before we leave, I should mention one more very important kind of service the computer provides in this plant. Do you notice that many of the people who work here are wearing those round metal hats and those funny plastic glasses?

Right. In any plant or factory, there's often the danger of explosions, or hot chemicals being spilled, or electrical shocks. So safety controls are very important.

How does the computer help with this?

Since computers are always measuring temperatures and pressures and levels, they can set off alarms whenever one of these things reaches a danger point. They flash messages on the terminal screens, ring alarm bells, even shut down all the systems that are causing the danger.

If there's a fire, the computer can turn a sprinkler system on, and shut all the doors and windows around the danger area. Some even notify the fire department.

I wish we had something like that in my house.

Some people already do. And maybe someday everyone will. Right now, it's time for our next stop.

W*here are we going now?*

Well, how about a short shopping trip?

Shopping? What do we need to buy?

Nothing, really. But it might be interesting to see how things are being bought and sold these days. We'll start with this department store.

Let's go over to the cash register, where that man is buying an umbrella. Do you see what the sales clerk is doing?

Look closely at the price tag. See all those black bars printed there—some fat ones and some thin ones, all in a row?

Yes. They're on all the price tags.

Right. Those bars are a sort of code—each pattern is different and tells us what the item is and how much it costs.

It does? But I can't read a bunch of bars!

But those pens can. When the clerk moves the pen across the bars, the price of that umbrella appears in that window across the top of the cash register.

I'll bet I know how those pens read the bars.

By now, I'm sure you do.

It's like those sensors we saw in the factory that measured how hot or cold or full a tank was. They were connected to a computer, and I'll bet those pens are, too.

Right you are. The computer, as usual, has all the necessary information stored about each item in the store—the whole inventory.

What's an inventory?

That means how many of each item the store has for sale. Those pens not only read the price, but they tell the computer what item a customer is buying, so the computer can subtract one from the inventory. That way, the store always knows how many they've got left.

And every time someone buys an umbrella, or a hat, or a dress, or a pair of shoes, the computer always changes the inventory for that item. Then when the number gets too low, it prints a message to the storekeeper to place an order for some more.

Just like the factory computer told the engineer when the temperature was getting too hot or cold.

Exactly. Now, the man is ready to pay for his umbrella. See what he's giving to the clerk?

But do you know how that little piece of plastic pays for things?

Each credit card has a code printed on it, just like the price tags. And the bank that issued the card has a computer that knows which code belongs to each of its customers.

When the store sends this credit card code to the bank, along with the price of the item being bought, the bank's computer figures out the bill and sends the customer a statement at the end of the month.

Now, let's go to a different kind of store. It's just down the street . . .

. . . and here we are at the grocery store.

It sure is crowded.

And that usually means long lines at the check-out counter. But computers are helping to make this part of shopping a lot faster and smoother. See what the clerks are doing with each item from the shopping carts?

Correct. And do you see the small black bars printed on that box of cornflakes? And on that package of meat?

Just like the price tags in the department store! There's one on that loaf of bread . . . and that jar of peanut butter. But . . . where's the pen that reads them?

Under that plate of glass. It's a little beam of light that shines up and reads the bars as the food item passes across. The computer figures out the price and displays it on the cash register. Then it adds everything together.

It's a lot faster than pushing keys on the cash register and it doesn't make mistakes. The clerk can bag the groceries at the same time as the computer reads the prices, instead of having to do it all afterward.

Now we could go on to almost any other store and see the same thing. Even lots of small shops have their own small, inexpensive computers. But it's time to go to our next stop. And we'll have to take the subway.

Good! I like riding on the subway.

Sure, because it's fast and convenient. Thanks to computers.

You mean subways use computers, too?

Of course. Remember how the computer decided where each police car should go, so that all parts of the city were patrolled?

Yes—and it always knew where each one was, in case of an emergency.

Right. Well, subways work the same way. The computer knows how many subway trains there are going in each direction, how many cars each one has, and where they have to stop to let passengers on and off. Can you imagine what would happen if each train went anywhere it wanted and as fast as it wanted?

They'd be running into each other all the time!

They sure would. And if one train breaks down somewhere, the computer has to make sure the ones behind it take a different track or wait till it can get moving again.

The computer also makes sure more trains run more often during rush hour, when people are going to and from work. And it can send fewer trains late at night or on weekends when not so many people need them.

Also, some subways, like this one, use computers to figure out how much to charge passengers for rides. See these little tickets? They have codes on them, just like the code bars in the stores we visited.

As we go through the gate, we put the ticket into this little slot, where a beam of light reads the code. When we get off the train, the ticket goes into another slot, and the computer figures out how far we've gone and how much to charge.

What about things like buses, taxis and airplanes? Do they use computers, too?

Most definitely. Almost all forms of public transportation use computers to plan schedules, routes and charges. Especially the airlines, as we will now see . . . because here we are at the airport.

Boy, it's a busy place, too.

Sure is. At any time of the day or night, there are thousands of people up in the air, coming from or going to somewhere. It's a big job to make sure they all arrive and leave on time, get to the right place and pay the right amount. . . .

I know what you're going to say! It's computers that do all those things!

You guessed it. See those terminals at the check-in counters? They're connected to computers that know how many planes each airline has, where each of them goes and what time they leave and arrive.

It also knows how many passengers each one can hold and how many people have already bought tickets. And if there's no direct flight available to some city, the computer can figure out how to reroute passengers so they end up in the right place.

But the computer does a lot more than just handle reservations. Let's go up to the flight control deck. . . .

You'll see why in a minute. This is where the flight controllers—and computers—stay in contact with the planes while they're in flight, and supervise takeoffs and landings. The traffic controllers are sort of like patrol car dispatchers at the police station.

See those lights on that big glass screen? Those represent planes in flight between here and other cities. The computer knows just where they are by the radar signals they send, and it draws a picture of each plane on the screen so the flight controllers will know, too. That's why it's dark in here—so the planes on the screen will show up better.

What are those numbers written next to the marks for the planes?

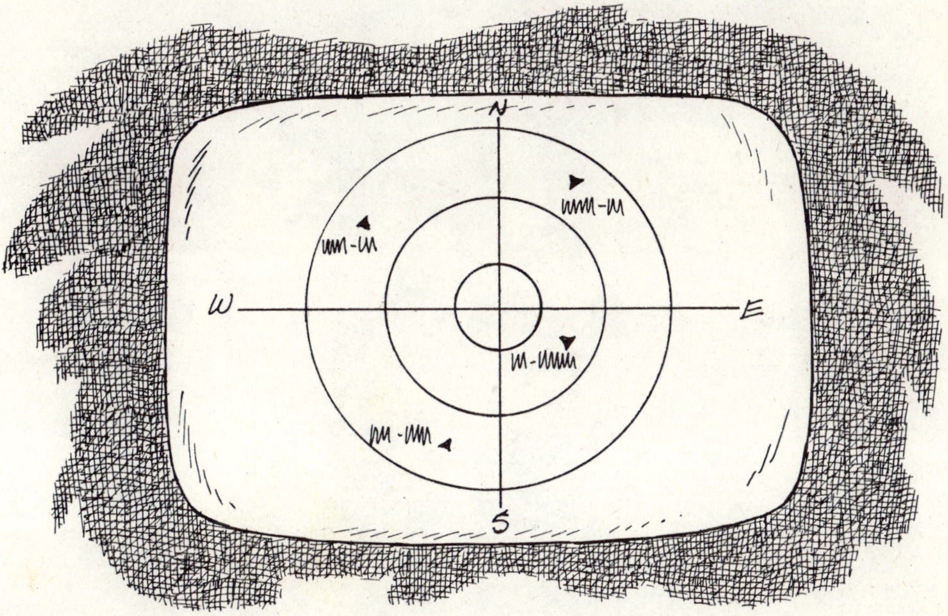

Those are the airplane's identification code, altitude and speed. If a plane is in trouble or off course, the flight controllers will know it right away.

Now, besides the computers here at the airport, each plane has its own computer in the cockpit to give the pilot information about his speed, altitude, direction and fuel. The computer can fly the plane automatically during parts of the flight.

I guess it would be hard to get anywhere without computers.

Well, people did it once. But not as often and they usually didn't go very far or very fast.

And even today, most people drive cars, which don't need computers . . . although that is already changing, too.

But the farther we go, and the faster we go, the more computers are necessary. That's why the space program could not even exist without them.

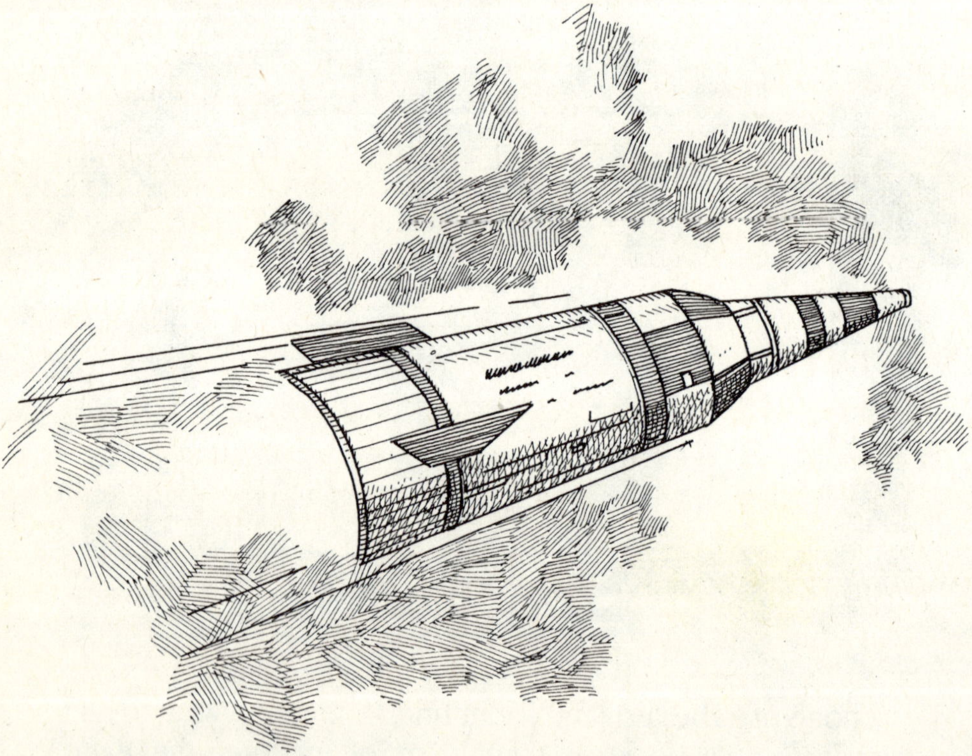

The Voyagers and Pioneers, flying out there beyond Jupiter and Saturn, depend on computers to guide them, and to gather information to send back to Earth.

The space shuttle has four computers to do all those things airplane computers do, plus other jobs like launching satellites and performing scientific experiments in space.

And all those moon landings—from launching, to orbiting the moon, separating the landing module, landing on the moon, taking off from the moon, returning to Earth and final splashdown—every mile of the way the astronauts were always depending on their computers.

Well, do you think you've seen enough?

Enough? You mean there's still more?

Oh, we could go on and on. We could go to the telephone company and see how computers are used to handle all those millions of calls that go on all the time. Or how they tell you when a number has been changed. Or how they add up long-distance charges for your monthly bill.

Or we could go to the Pentagon near Washington, D.C. to see how computers are used to plan defense strategies

in case of an attack. Or how they're used to break enemy codes. Or how they detect and identify enemy airplanes, submarines and even missiles.

Or we could see how computers are used to check books in and out of the library, to control traffic lights on busy streets, to sort mail in the post office, to help teach schoolchildren to add and subtract, to protect your home against fire and burglary, to help farmers raise better crops and animals, to—

Okay, I'm convinced. There's just one thing I want to know.

Yes, what's that?

How did people get along before there were any computers?

Do you know, people used to ask the same thing about television . . . and telephones . . . and cars. . . .

Yes, but those things have been around for years and years.

Mmmm . . . not all *that* long. Besides, computers have been around for a while, too.

Then why has everybody suddenly started talking about them?

Because it's only been in the last few years that computers have been small enough, fast enough and cheap enough for everybody to use them. And some had to be the size of a truck just to do anything at all! And they cost millions of dollars to make.

Really? What were they like? Did they have terminals? And use light pens and sensors?

No, those things came much later. One of the first computers to become famous was called ENIAC. It was built about fifty years ago and it looked like this:

It had thousands of vacuum tubes, and—

What's a vacuum tube?

A vacuum tube was what computers used to store information. They were sort of like light bulbs that turned on and off and they were always burning out, so they had to be replaced constantly. But the first real computers all used vacuum tubes.

What do you mean real computers? Were there some that weren't real?

By real computer, I mean one that works by electricity. And yes, there were some even before that. They were powered by hand, or even by steam. But they never worked very well.

So everybody just had to do all their figuring with a pencil and paper.

Oh, no—don't forget about the *slide rule* and the *abacus.*

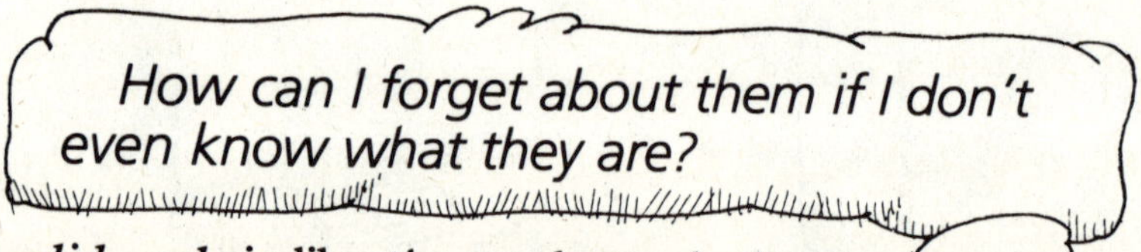

Okay. A *slide rule* is like the pocket calculators you see today, except that it is worked by hand.

The slide rule has a middle section that slides back and forth, matching up the numbers you want to add or subtract. When you get the numbers lined up, you read the answers on another part of the scale.

It's a lot easier just to push some buttons on my pocket calculator.

Yes, it is. But some mathematicians are so good with the slide rule that they can get their answers faster than someone with a calculator.

An *abacus* is an earlier version of the slide rule . . . thousands of years old, in fact. It has rods strung with beads, and the beads can be moved around in order to add and subtract. The old abacus operators were so fast you could hardly see their fingers fly.

But the slide rule and the abacus aren't really computers, are they?

That depends. The word "compute" means to use mathematics to solve problems. Today's computers do a lot more than that, as you have already seen. But the slide rule and abacus have helped people to count and solve arithmetic problems, so maybe we should call them computers, too.

Were there any computers before the abacus?

Oh, yes. People used piles of stones or sticks to count and even carry out simple arithmetic.

I mean a computer that you could carry around with you.

Yes, indeed. In fact, man has been carrying a computer around with him about as long as he's been here on Earth.

Really? What did it look like?

Well, it's grey, about the size of a cantaloupe and weighs about three pounds.

Huh? People carried that around with them?

They still do. Everyone has one, including you.

I do? Where?

Right up there . . . inside your head.

Indeed I am. It may not be the smallest computer in the world or even the fastest. But so far, it's still the best.

I never thought my brain was a computer.

Oh, yes. Computers used to be called "electronic brains." In fact, your whole body is like a complete computer system—it works very much the same way.

What's a computer system?

A computer system is everything a computer needs to do its job. For instance, where does a computer get its power to run?

Electricity.

Right. So does your brain. Your body contains chemicals that produce tiny amounts of electricity that the brain uses to work. Also, the brain needs oxygen—

It gets oxygen from blood! We learned that in school.

Right again. Computers, of course, don't need oxygen, but they do need to be kept clean and at the right temperature, and that's something else the blood does for the brain. Now, what else does a computer need?

What else? Gee . . . I'm not sure.

I'll give you a hint. Suppose I told you to add 2 and 2 on a pocket calculator. What would you do?

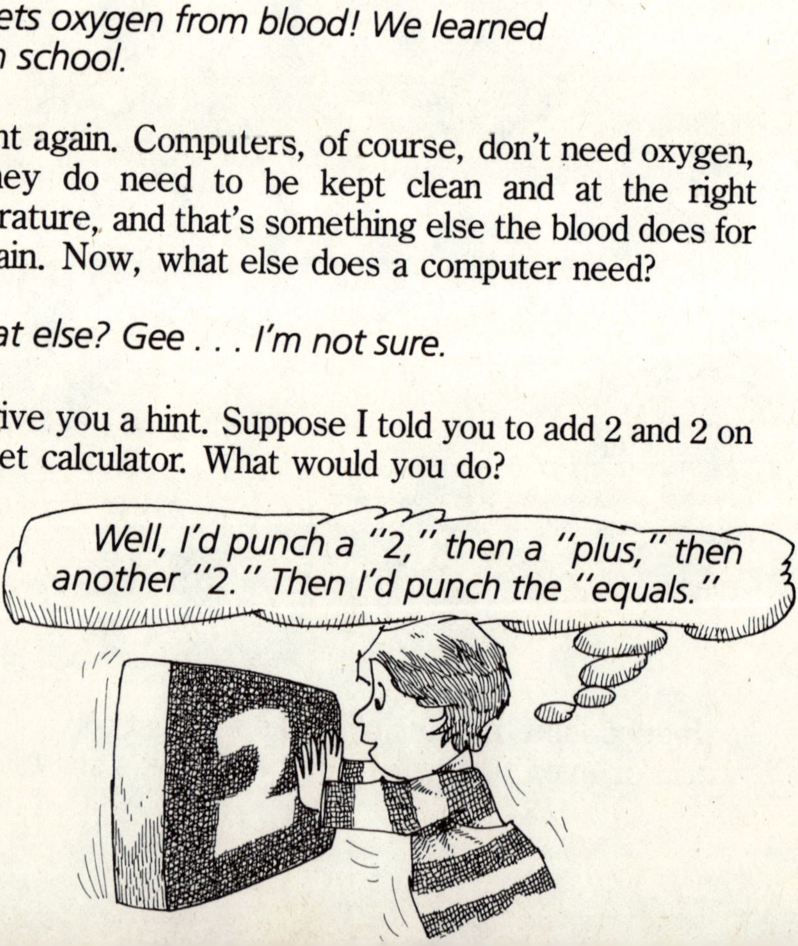

Right. Would the calculator add the numbers if you didn't punch the keys?

In fact, how would it even know to add instead of subtract, or multiply, or divide? You had to tell it, right? By pushing the buttons.

Right.

So the other thing a computer needs is information—what numbers to use and what to do with them.

Oh, I see! Like the information they typed in at the hospital and at the police station.

Correct. And this information has a name. We call it *input.*

But what about my brain? If it's a computer, it needs input, too.

Of course. If I expect you to add 2 and 2, I have to give your brain this input.

But there aren't any buttons to push on my head. How does the input get put in?

Well, it got there, didn't it? Don't you remember how?

Right! Your ears hear my instructions and the numbers I say aloud. And this information, this input, goes to your brain. Just like pushing buttons on a calculator.

Now, there are lots of other ways input gets to your brain. Can you think of any?

Correct. If you saw the numbers 2 and 2 written on a piece of paper, along with the word ADD, you'd know exactly what to do.

But a computer can't hear or see.

Actually, some of them can. But they're very special. Most computers get their input from a set of keys on a terminal, like the ones we saw in all those places we visited. You push them just like the buttons on a pocket calculator and the information gets sent over wires to the computer.

I don't have wires in my head, do I?

Sure you do. They're called *nerves*, and they carry messages and information from your ears and eyes right to your brain. In fact, nerves run to all parts of your body, bringing all kinds of input to the brain.

Your fingers feel something rough or smooth, or hot or cold, or wet, or sharp, or lumpy.

Your nose smells something spicy, or flowery, or stinky.

Your tongue tastes something sweet, or sour, or bitter, or salty.

Exactly. It travels along those wires called nerves to tell the brain what's happening around it.

That's even better than pushing buttons or typing on keys!

True, but remember I said some computers can see. And some can hear. And some can even feel.

You mean they have eyes and ears and fingers?

Almost. A camera, for example, can take pictures and send them to the computer, like our eyes do for the brain. Remember the Voyager pictures of Saturn? They were sent through a computer first.

And you know those beeps a telephone makes when you push the buttons? A computer "hears" those tones and connects you to the right number.

Remember the sensors in the chemical plant? They were the "fingers" that felt the temperature in the tank and told the computer when the stuff inside was getting too hot or too cold.

So you see, input to a computer can be pretty much the same as it is to the brain.

Except I'll bet there aren't any computers that can smell or taste.

Well . . . I won't say there aren't. But they'd be pretty special, indeed!

Okay, now you said my brain was just like a computer. And I see where brains and computers get their input. But that's just the in part. Where does the input get put?

Good question. Let's talk about your brain first and see where things get put in there.

Inside, there are millions and millions of *cells*. Do you know what cells are?

I think so. In school, we learned that all living things are made up of cells, so tiny you need a microscope to see them. And there are all different kinds—skin cells, bone cells, blood cells. . . .

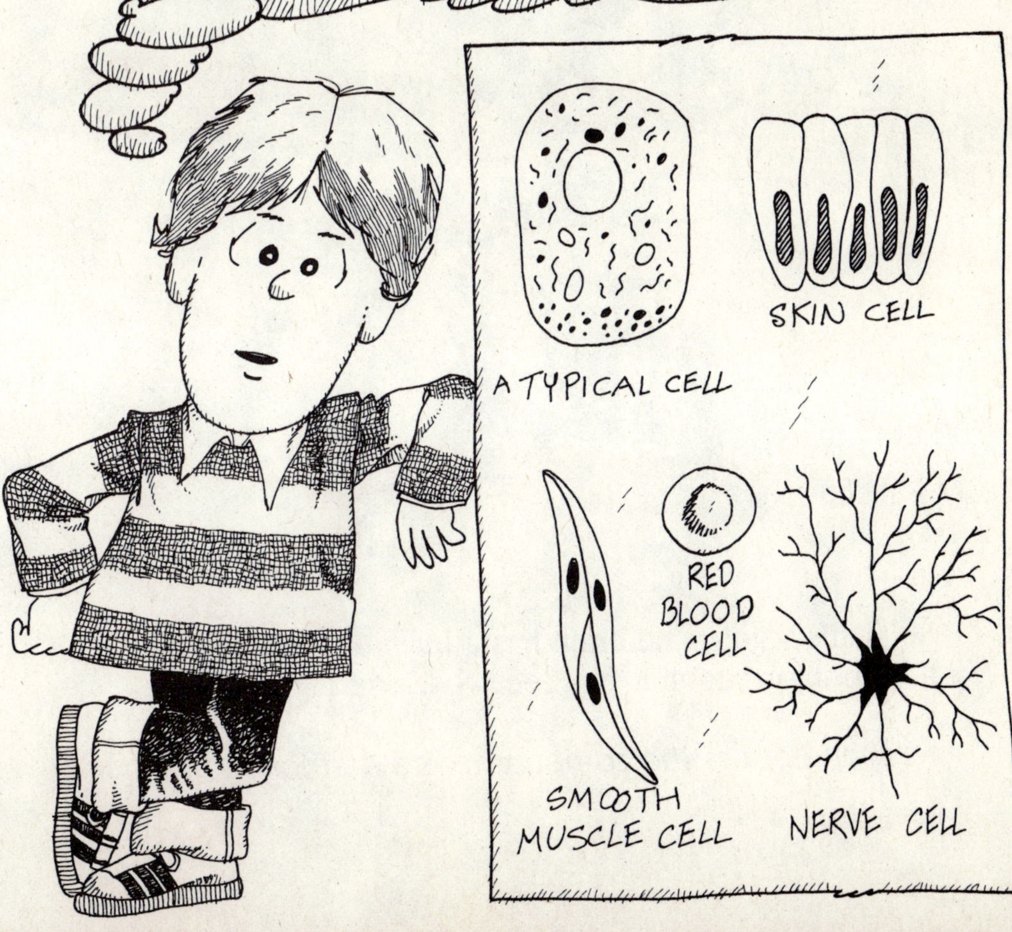

And *brain cells.* These are very special cells that can hold information. This is where input to your brain is kept. Can you guess what this part of the brain is called?

Give me a hint.

Okay. When you take a test in school, and you have to *remember* all the things you've learned, you'd better have a good _ _ _ _ _ _ _.

That's right. The brain has a *memory* so it won't forget all the information it has received.

Then I guess the computer has a memory, too.

Certainly does. The input to a computer is stored in its memory until it's ready to be used. Later on, we'll see what a computer memory looks like and how it works.

But remembering is not all a brain does, is it?

It's not?

Of course not. If I gave you several numbers to add, I'd expect you to do more than just remember the numbers!

Oh, I see! So the computer has to be able to add, too.

And subtract, and divide, and multiply, and all the other things a brain can do . . . and a few more complicated ones as well. In other words, it has to *do* something with its input. This is called *processing* because it goes through a *process*, or steps, to get an answer.

Yes, it does. To find the sum of several numbers, you add the first two together, then add the third to that, then add the fourth, the fifth, and so on. And when the sums of the numbers you're adding are bigger than 10, you have to *carry.*

Each of those steps is part of the process. A computer does everything in lots of short steps, so we call it processing.

But there's more to processing than just adding and subtracting numbers.

Like what?

Suppose there were two good television programs you wanted to see, but they were on at the same time.

Exactly. You have to make a *decision.* You do it all the time. Should you wear your blue sweater or your brown one? Should you walk to a friend's house or ride your bike? Should you have a pepperoni pizza or a cheese pizza?

Okay—but that's still a decision your brain has to make. And a computer has to make decisions, too.

When sensors send temperature information to the computer, the computer has to decide when to turn on the heat and when to turn it off. The computer in an airplane or spacecraft has to decide when to increase speed or slow down, and when to turn and which way to turn.

Now. Let's see if you can remember all those things we've been talking about. Information that goes into a computer is called _ _ _ _ _.

Input!

And it's stored in the computer's _ _ _ _ _ _.

Memory!

And when the computer uses that information it's called _ _ _ _ _ _ _ _ _ _ _.

Processing!

And in processing, the computer has to make _ _ _ _ _ _ _ _ _ _.

Decisions!

You score 100%! Very good!

But now there's one more very important thing we haven't mentioned. In fact, without it, none of these other things would do us any good at all!

What's that?

Well, let's go back to the brain, and our addition example. If I tell you to add some numbers, and your brain figures out the answer, how am I going to know what it *is*, unless—

Unless I tell you!

Right! What good are answers unless you can tell someone what they are?

Now, if the information I put *in* to your brain is called *input*, what do you suppose we'd call the information your brain puts back *out* to me?

It must be output.

I knew you'd get that one. Now, how does this *output* get from your brain to me?

That's one way. Can you think of any other ways?

So output is a lot like input—there are all kinds of different ways of getting the information in and the answers out.

How does the computer do it?

I thought you'd never ask. A computer can do it in several ways, too. Remember the terminals that were used to send input to the computer?

Yes.

Well, they can also be used to receive output. A computer can send its answers right back to the screen on the same terminal. Or any other terminal screen, for that matter. Can you think of some examples from our visits?

Sure. At the hospital, the information about the patients came up on the screen. And in the police car, the information about license plate numbers.

Good. Now, another way a computer can give us output is by typing on a *printer.* A printer is like a terminal, but it has a long stream of paper instead of a screen, so you can pull it out, tear it off and take it with you.

What about talking? Can a computer tell you the output, like I tell you the answers to the arithmetic problem?

Some computers can. When you punch a number on the telephone, a computer uses an operator's voice to tell you if the number has been changed and to give you the new number.

Now, there's another kind of output that the computer uses, which doesn't necessarily print or tell you anything. Instead, it makes something happen.

Like what?

Remember the chemical plant, where the tanks had to be heated to just the right temperature?

Sure, and the computer was hooked up to the tanks to measure the temperatures.

Now, what would we call the temperatures that were sent to the computer?

Input.

And what happened when the computer saw that the temperatures were too high or too low?

It changed a color picture on a terminal screen to show the engineers what was happening.

And that was the. . . .

But the computer also did something else, remember?

Oh, yes! It sent a signal back to the tank to turn a heater up or down to make the temperature correct.

And do you remember what that was called?

Process control.

Correct. And *process control* is another kind of output. Computers can control speeds and directions and pressures and all kinds of things.

Again, it's just like what your brain does. Instead of telling you to add two numbers, suppose I told you to open the door. What does your brain do?

Right. It controls your arm and fingers and wrist.

So now we've talked about input, output, memory, processing, decisions and control. Have you seen any difference between the way your brain does these things and the way a computer does them?

I can't think of any. So why do we need computers? Aren't there enough brains to do all the things computers do?

Sure there are. In fact, brains have to design and build the computers in the first place. But computers are used where brains would be wasted.

Wasted?

Well, would you want to sit around all day just adding up millions of numbers, or making temperatures go up and down?

But computers don't get bored. And they can add those numbers a lot faster, and control those temperatures a lot more exactly, than any brain.

I'll bet they can remember better, too. I sometimes forget things.

Well, computers don't exactly forget things, but their memories are very tiny compared to the brain's.

They are?

Certainly. Somewhere in your brain's memory, everything you have ever learned, or read, or seen, is stored. There's so much that you can't ever remember it all.

A computer's memory is very small, but it can always remember everything that's in there.

No, they wouldn't forget. And computer memories are getting bigger. But they're very expensive, and take up a lot of space. So computers use some other things to help them remember.

Like what?

Well, what do you do in school when your brain can't remember everything the teacher is saying?

So does a computer. It remembers all the important things, the information it needs right away and has to use often. But most of it gets written onto a kind of notebook called a *disk*.

A disk?

That's right. It looks like a record album—it even comes in a cover for protection. It fits into a *disk drive*, like your record player, and spins very fast. It can hold thousands of times more information than the computer's memory.

And when a computer needs some of that information, a small device, like the needle on a record player tone arm, reads it from the disk and sends it to the computer.

Is that another kind of input?

It is. Input can come from a disk as well as from a terminal or a sensor.

How does the information get on the disk in the first place?

For that, just the opposite happens. Whenever the computer needs to save some information, or doesn't have room for it in its memory, it sends it out to the disk—just like it sends signals out to the tank of chemicals to control the temperature. And just like when you write down things in your notebook. And it stays there until it's needed.

So then that's another kind of output.

Correct. Instead of being printed or used to control a process, output can be saved, or *stored,* on a disk. That's why we call a disk a *storage device.*

Are there any other kinds of storage devices?

Yes, there are. Do you know what a tape recorder looks like?

Sure—it's a box with a long ribbon that winds from one wheel to another one, and plays music and things like a record player.

Okay. That box is called a *tape drive,* the wheels are called *tape reels,* and the ribbon is called *magnetic tape.* Information can be stored on that tape just like on a disk. As the tape moves from one reel to the other, the computer can read the information from it or put new information back on to it.

A tape isn't as fast as a disk, but it can store even more information. It's more complete, like an encyclopedia, while a disk is like the notebook that you carry with you and use more often. And of course computer memory keeps the information it needs all the time—it's right there, ready to use immediately.

Just like the brain.

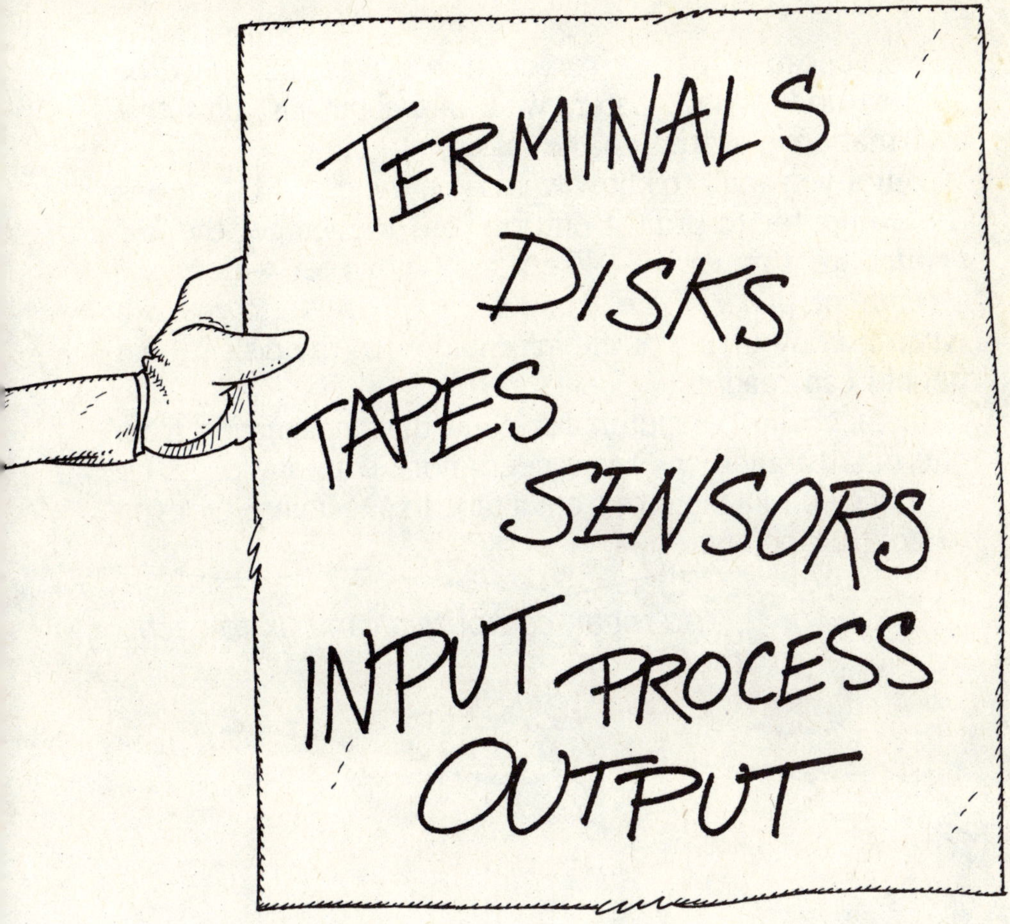

Just like the brain. And that's what we've been talking about all this time, isn't it? That the computer is just like the brain.

And a whole computer *system*—with terminals and disks and tapes and sensors—is like your whole body, where the brain lives. It uses its "eyes" and "ears" and "fingers" for input and output. It can control processes, and it can even store information to use whenever it is needed.

What if people want to know what information is on the disk? Can they just listen to it, like I listen to a record?

No, because it's not recorded in a way that you'd be able to understand. Later, we'll talk about just how that information is stored on the disk.

But if you want to know what is on the disk, you can ask the computer to print it out for you. Remember the *line printer* we saw earlier—like a big typewriter with a long stream of paper? The computer can use it to make a written copy of any of the information on the disk so that people can read it.

In fact, the computer can copy that information from one disk to another, if you need more than one copy. Or from a disk to a tape, or from a tape to a terminal. Or even to another computer.

Sure. If a whole computer system is really going to be like a person, it should be able to exchange its information with other computers, just like you do with your friends. You tell them things you know and they tell you things they know.

This is called a *computer network*. You know what a net is, don't you?

Of course. It's lots of string or ropes all connected together.

Well, that's what a computer network is—lots of computers connected together. But they don't even have to be in the same place. They can talk to each other over telephone lines because telephone lines are all connected together.

Yes, it is. And libraries, for example. If one library doesn't have the book you want, you can usually get it from another library that's on the same network.

And if one computer gets "sick," another computer on its network can sometimes take its place for a while.

You mean computers can get sick, just like people?

That's right. Things can go wrong with a computer, just like they can with the body. Something can break, like when you break an arm or a leg. Or if the power goes off, a computer can't work, although some of them have batteries that they can use until the power comes back on.

But all the important computers—like the ones in a spacecraft—have *back-ups* that can take their place if they have a problem. Like an actor in a play who gets sick—there's always a back-up so the show can go on.

I guess computers have to have doctors then, too.

By all means. A computer "doctor" is an engineer whose job it is to keep the computer working by checking it regularly and to fix it if anything does go wrong.

A person stays healthy by getting plenty of exercise, eating good food, staying clean and getting enough sleep. A computer doesn't eat or sleep, but it may have to run for days or weeks at a time. So it's important to watch for signs of problems. Some computers can even tell you when something is starting to go wrong.

They can?

Sure. Just like your own body does. When your temperature starts to go up, your body is telling you that something is wrong and that you need to take medicine or call a doctor. A computer can type a message, or turn on a warning light . . . and often can tell the engineer just where the problem is.

It's hard to believe a computer can do all that.

But it's true. In fact, there are really no limits to the things that computers can accomplish. That's why we keep inventing new sizes, shapes and flavors. We're always trying to get them to do things they've never done before.

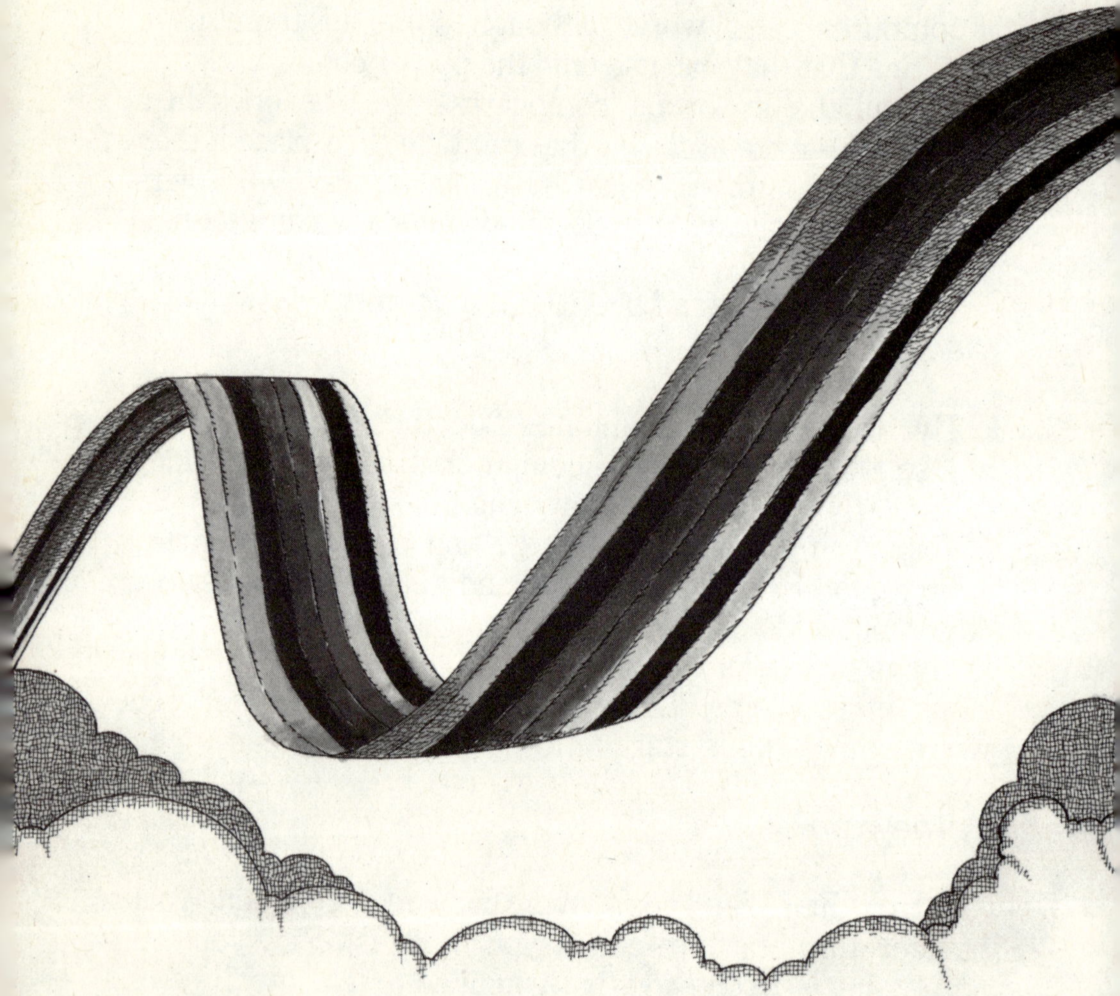

GLOSSARY

Computer system — All the equipment necessary for a computer to receive, store, process and produce information.

Disk — A device resembling a record album, used to store large amounts of information that will be used by a computer or that have been produced by a computer.

Input — Information which is put into a computer for storage or processing.

Memory — The part of a computer that stores information while it is being processed.

Network — A collection of computers in different locations that can exchange information, usually over telephone lines or by satellite.

Output — Information transferred out of a computer for display, storage or control.

Processing — Operations performed by a computer to provide information requested by a user.

Process control — The use of computers to direct the actions of machinery or operations in a factory or plant.

Sensor — A small device that measures temperatures, pressures or other physical properties.

Tape — A reel of magnetic ribbon used to store large amounts of information that will be used by a computer or that have been produced by a computer.

Terminal — A piece of equipment with a typewriter keyboard and video screen, used for communicating with a computer.